Hurricane Lamp

Phoenix Poets
A series edited by Robert von Hallberg

Hurricane Lamp
Turner Cassity

The University of Chicago Press
Chicago and London

TURNER CASSITY was born in 1929 in Jackson, Mississippi. He attended Millsaps College, Stanford University, and Columbia University before receiving his education in the U.S. Army and the South African Civil Service. Mr. Cassity is currently catalog librarian at the R. W. Woodruff Library, Emory University.

The University of Chicago Press, Chicago 60637
The University of Chicago Press, Ltd., London

© 1986 by The University of Chicago
All rights reserved. Published 1986
Printed in the United States of America

95 94 93 92 91 90 89 88 87 86   5 4 3 2 1

Library of Congress Cataloging-in-Publication Data

Cassity, Turner.
    Hurricane lamp.

    (Phoenix poets)
    I. Title. II. Series.
PS3553.A8H8   1986   811'.54   85-20873
ISBN 0-226-09614-9
ISBN 0-226-09615-7 (pbk.)

It is so shocking for cruelty to be unconscious. It makes it seem so deep and ingrained, as if it might lead to anything. And I believe it does. I once read a wicked book, called a school story.

—I. Compton-Burnett, *Elders and Betters*

These poems first appeared in the following publications:

Chattahoochee Review. "After the Fall"
Chicago Review. "The Garden and the Gods," "A Dance Part Way around the Veau d'Or," "A Salutation to the Moons of Saturn," "Hurricane Lamp," "Seeking a Level," "News for Loch Ness," "Relics"
Crazy Horse. "Maeterlinck in Ontario"
Cumberland Poetry Review. "Do Not Judge by Appearances. Or Do," "The Chinaberry Tree," "Eniwetok Mon Amour"
Georgia Review. "Elijah of the Backward Glance"
Gramercy Review. "The Miller," "At the Mercy of the Queen-Empress," "A Song for Clines Corners"
Greensboro Review. "Flying Friendly Skies," "Hunting," "Page from a Bar Guide"
Iowa Review. "The Goblin Market"
Nebo. "To the Lighthouse"
Parnassus. "Promises, Promises"
Poetry Miscellany. "Via Spaceship through Saskatchewan"
Ploughshares. "U-24 Anchors off New Orleans"
Poetry. "Why Fortune is the Empress of the World," "The Strange Case of Dr. Jekyll and Dr. Jekyll," "Two Are Four," "Morning on the Dodecanese Boulevard," "A Dialogue with the Bride of Godzilla," "Imputations," "The Aswan Rowing Club," "Cendrillon," "Ghosts," "I the Swineherd," "Our Lady's Juggler," "In the Kingdom of Jerusalem," "Favors," "The Space between the Andirons"
Renaissance. "Scheherazade in South Dakota," "Advice to King Lear"
Roberson Poetry Annual. "Dispensations of the Date Fairy," "Presence Française," "The Alfano Ending"
Southern Poetry Review. "The New Dolores Leather Bar," "Adding Rattles"
The Southern Review. "Pausing in the Climb," "Appalachia in Cincinnati," "Death and the Bush Pilot," "Anastasia," "A Distant View of the Chinese Wall," "Wine from the Cape"
Yale Review. "Berolina Demodée"

The writer would like to express his appreciation to the National Endowment for the Arts, with the aid of a grant from whom this volume was completed.

Contents

Do Not Judge by Appearances. Or Do.

The children of the crossing bear their sleep
Still with them, like another instrument
To weight them down; a shadow of the French horn,
Say; a heavy nimbus of the trombone.
Their cases miss the concrete of the walk
Exactly, as their noses the exact
Height of their turned-up collars. Now two more
Have joined them. Athletes, on the evidence
Of ditty bags and shoes, and wide awake.
The crossing guard is Ilse Koch, or if
She isn't ought to be: a leather cap
And body of a lampshade. Competent,
But not whom one would hire as sitter twice.
Will it be always their perception that,
Bold, safety wears the garb of violence?
Or will they learn in these too guarded streets
That pretty is as pretty does, but evil
May in fact be just as evil looks?
The final irresponsibility
Is never to impute, and all they know,
For now, is that the holster is a case
And what it holds is merely instrument,
No agent in the fight they fight. The trombone
Has attacked the ditty duo. Ilse,
In a world she both enjoys and knows,
Stops traffic and moves in to separate.

1

Why Fortune is the Empress of the World

The insect born of royalty has Marx
And worker housing as a life; has sex
Or clover honey to his pleasure, as
Have we. The parrot speaks. All use: the ant
The aphid and the crocodile the bird.
What then is human wholly? Is it heart?
Fidelity exists in any dog.
Good Doctor who have found your Missing Link,
On your return what will you have him be?
Free agent or a tenant in a cage?

A simple test will serve. It more or less
Is this: can he be taught a game of chance?
It is not possible, you must agree,
To think of animals as gambling. Odds,
Except for us, do not exist. An ape
Assumes always his jump will reach the limb.
For all his skill, he cannot cut his loss.
We, on the other hand, at our most threatened
Turn instinctively . . . to Reason? No.
To Fortune, as a mindlessness of mind.
The random that we create creates us.
In overcrowded lifeboats, we draw lots.

A Dance Part Way around the Veau d'Or, or, Rich within the Dreams of Avarice

You poor, dependable, discreet small Mammon!
Had you form, what might it be? How summon

Arms of Moloch or the golden calf
If you are too exiguous by half?

A stripper's falsies, say? Transvestite's egret?
You are my dirty little open secret.

You prevent me, truth who act as sham,
From tribute as the worker that I am.

For gifts in childhood, my backhanded Baal,
Thank you. Your rebate let me countervail;

As in my busy, happy adolescence
You, the silent, stubborn, growing presence,

Sacrificed. I also thank you, center—
Part rather—of my being, for my winter

Each second year vacations. Cross I bear,
How I enjoy your stations! I, sole heir

Of that penurious young scare I was,
Gain now the ruby slippers. Eat cake, Oz.

Inflated quackery the tin ear praises,
Lionizer whom the lion dazes,

Ease the youth of whom you hit upon.
You are yourself what I now spit upon.

Income unearned, I say I'm quite above you.
In point of fact I love you, love you, love you.

Reinventing the Alphabet

Palamedes . . . invented consonants; and Hermes reduced these
sounds to characters, using wedge shapes because cranes fly in
wedge formation.
                    —Robert Graves, *The Greek Myths*

> So slow
> You go,
>
> High jet,
> You let
>
> One score
> Once more
>
> On clear,
> Wax air
>
> What? Greek?
> A streak
>
> Of runes?
> Intense
>
> Cyril-
> lic spell,
>
> Is Chi
> On sky
>
> All speech
> You teach?
>
> A blue,
> Void view
>
> Its word
> Interred?

Flying Friendly Skies

Our left and right show red and green: mute phonics.
A two-light Christmas in a sky of onyx,
The 1011 is an hour from Phoenix.

The cabin lights are off, and at my side
A sleeping Pfc., his waking bride,
Have heads an airline pillow may divide,

But somewhat as a cut divides the cards—
In no essential. Having knitted yards,
My neighbor on the other side—her guard's

Up always—draws a game of solitaire.
"The point of Phoenix," says she, "is its *air*."
Sun City is for her the at, the where.

The two young people near the primal scene.
The solitary, tactful, has to screen
Her reading light. I? I fall in between.

Dispensations of the Date Fairy
(Death Valley)

In drier air than tongue can wet
I buy this sack of dates and eat.

Oasis each, each has its dust.
An eye has moisture; grapes have frost.

And as a thinnest frost of ice
Tonight will sparkle in their trees,

These warm confections of the palm,
Left on the sill outside my room,

Must match the grape for blue and cold.
It is to eat the sun grown old,

As, in the skies of Furnace Creek
High furnaces of stars burn black

The sky behind them—diamond
That air and diamond the land.

I take the diamonds on trust.
I feel my lips stick on the dust.

The Garden and the Gods

Site of the world famous Easter sunrise service, the bizarre
spines and pinnacles have been ranked in degree of difficulty for
climbers.
—*A.A.A. paragraph on Colorado Springs*

Field glasses on the cocktail terrace, I,
Rock climbers in my figure eighted sky.

Long tenure, you, and if your handhold fails
Be where you fall (the figure eight avails)

Outside my field of vision. Why then watch?
To learn the look of what is mostly touch.

Practitioner that on the living rock
To your own ego nail yourself, no look

Of mine can teach you how to miss your thorns,
Or trust the nails, or move at last the stone.

The scrutiny that learns, its lenses hood,
And with it or without, well understood

For will triumphant, misconstrued as trust,
You equally are exhibitionist.

The coin runs out; dark shutters end your hour.
Ego, I have no nine-and-twenty more.

Out of this barren garden, then, to air
Whose gifts or whose embrace are not my care,

Go up in ignorance. As much informed
As mind's stigmatic purposes demand,

My feel for bleeding palms, for height will pass.
The cocktail and the cup, alike, will pass.

Pausing in the Climb

Sun on the cheekbone like a razor cut,
Vein at the temple pounding.
Brilliant in the altitude
Volcanic sand; a brilliant air surrounding.

And at the very barrier, the high
Vague cordon quarantining
Ether from the air below,
Shines out, as in the shrub's Mosaic burning,

A single thistle as a timberline.
It is the blood itself
Insistent on the edge of time;
The branching armature whose either half,

As in a scan, the prickling weed projects—
The one half red with air,
The other, tree of our defects,
Forever livid in the airless, near,

So formless blue. Unspeaking, burning blossom,
Crown upon the thorn,
Do beating heart within the bosom
And a clotting, cold inertia born

Beside it share one color, to invoke us
Future in a hush
Of purple? Will your image mock us
In the morning as a shaving brush?

The Strange Case of
Dr. Jekyll and Dr. Jekyll

I drink no potion. To the double life
I bring no goatish hint of the exotic,
Have no weight of guilt to offer; have,
For now, no chilling drive of the fanatic.

My fleshpots—give them credit for perception—
Know me as the slummer that I am,
As I know them for applied corruption.
What we are, to what we are we come,

And only too prepared to settle for it.
Commerce comforts, in these middle years,
Once one has learned the young do not abhor it.
Curious that hard cash and that sneers

Win out where youth and eagerness did not,
But wholeness in that age is antiseptic.
It is what one had instead of Hyde.
It also is the reason, not now cryptic,

That today I buy and do not plead.
Part capital, my cautious potion-sippers,
Wholly venture. There the surgeon's blade—
It cuts both ways—succeeds to Jack the Ripper's.

The New Dolores Leather Bar

I adjure thee, respond from thine altars,
Our Lady of Pain.
            —A.C. Swinburne

Not quite alone from night to night you'll find them.
Who need so many shackles to remind them
Must doubt that they are prisoners of love.

The leather creaks; studs shine; the chain mail jingles.
Shoulders act as other forms of bangles
In a taste where push has come to shove.

So far from hardhats and so near to Ziegfeld,
They, their costume, fail. Trees felled, each twig felled,
One sees the forest: Redneck Riding Hood's.

Does better-dear-to-eat-you drag, with basket,
Make the question moot? Go on and ask it.
Red, do you deliver, warm, the goods?

Or is the axle-grease, so butch an aura,
Underneath your nails in fact mascara?
Caution, lest your lie, your skin unscarred,

Profane these clanking precincts of the pain queen.
Numb with youth, an amateur procaine queen,
In the rite you lose the passage. Hard,

To know the hurt the knowledge. Command is late now,
Any offer master of your fate now.
You can, though won't, escape. Tarnishing whore,

So cheap your metal and so thin your armor,
Fifteen years will have you once more farmer.
Mammon values; earth and pain ignore.
Name your price and serve him well before.

Two Are Four

Night without attribute,
To which you bring all elements in turn:
Air intermittent in your throat;
Earth errant in your heart.
Bright water where your wet lips part
For fire I bring you, even as you burn.

Appalachia in Cincinnati

We who have bridged the river
Find our bridgehead comfortless:
A few square blocks forever;
Limits steel guitars express.

Beyond the surplus stores,
The pawnshops and the storefront missions,
Outer inner-cores,
Blacks pursue their own persuasions.

We, the heart of darkness,
From our beer-and-sawdust floors,
Look past the pavement slickness
Toward the rainy, sooty airs

Of lighted hills above.
You ever comfortable, your houses
Cantilevered wave
On wave above our poor successes,

Pull your drapes more tightly
Or descend from where you view,
Voyeurs, and do your slumming rightly.
Buy us breakfast. How

Exotic, here where necks
Are red and waitresses are minors,
Flannel lumberjackets,
Soulless food in all-night diners.

Occupied Ohio,
World that ends at Clifton Ridge,
World without end or I.O.
U. calls us from Suspension Bridge.

Watch with us one hour.
The second coffees cool, and, lucky,
We see wet skies clear.
Your sun comes to you from Kentucky.

Hunting

Deer season near the end; new boots
And red windbreaker for the red
Young man who, sipping on a beer,
Hunts in the hardwoods, hound ahead,
Alert. It is, for all his gear,
However, mistletoe he shoots.

Green as a serpent, in a sense
As deadly, shot off at its stem
The sought-for parasitic falls:
The Druid lure. Each in their time
Our sights are set for love, our halls
Hang out the call to violence.

Morning on the Dodecanese Boulevard
(Tarpon Springs)

The olive fails us, and the sea withdraws
    Its offer of the horse
To have us gather, as a last recourse,
    Far sponges for your faint applause.

On agitated floors, in weighted boots,
    Slick rubber shapes our skin.
Our bodies (warmer suits) may be within
    Pure Greek—Praxitilean moods—

Or may not be. Ashore, the coffee's Turk,
    The footstool Ottoman,
The cheap turquoise New Mexico. At one
    Weak point, unknown, the tide turns back

And is its opposite. The bitten coin
    Becomes the credit card.
Melon of Persia, foe we breakfast on,
    The slice is crescent; the rind is hard.

U-24 Anchors off New Orleans
(1938)

The only major city, one would hope,
Below the level of a periscope.
An air so wet, a sewer-damp so ill,
One had as well be under water still.

The muddy river cakes us, camouflages.
Maddened goats, my crew go off in barges.
At a distance—I do not refer
To feet and inches—I go too. To err

Defines the deckhands; not to is the Bridge.
Discretion is the sex of privilege.
The streetcars meet the levee four abreast;
I cleverly have picked the noisiest.

A mad mapmaker made this master plan,
To wring out, of his grid of streets, a fan.
One German restaurant, well meant but erring:
Ten kinds of shellfish; bouillabaisse; no herring.

Have my men fared better? Where they are
Becomes a high Weimar Republic bar.
There—lower Bourbonstrasse—lace and leather
Mingle in Louisiana weather.

Crack your whip, Old Harlot; pop your garter.
Who lives here is, by definition, martyr.
If I come back I'll think to pack libido.
For symbolism there will be torpedo.

Phaëthon

(Unter den Linden)

Of all the German-Greek,
I only keep my chic.

The other gods, in ruin
Have whatever Zion

Or whatever dusk
Old protocols may ask

Of elders. Youth and fire,
I harness my desire.

The quadriga whose freight
Holds down the Doric gate

I free to air. And beast
And god, to west from east

Lay down, without a name,
Divisive streets of flame.

All things that were, that are,
X-ray themselves and char;

Street lamps and corniced heights,
The lime trees' blazing lights

And black tall cinders. Day
Or wrath, I am the way,

The path. If I am truth,
Then deviance is youth.

Old order of our pains,
My Father, take the reins.

Berolina Demodée

Erich Mendelsohn's buildings on the Lehniner Platz are presently
occupied by a bowling alley and a supermarket.
        —M. Henning-Schefold, *Frühe Moderne in Berlin*

City without shadows, hail!
Hail, *ville radieuse*. Yet, here,

something—haze, perhaps, soot on
high steel, my own middle age—

creates, as I stroll idly,
its illusion of shadow.

Rounded concrete, chrome, windows
that round corners, strip-windows

banding eave to facade . . . these,
here and there, like a darkness,

shade the bright glass curtain walls.
Did they once, in their far time,

seem promise of a more far
travel? I pass a spaceport;

I look away. At my age
one does not see without pain

Blitz Gordon on the check-out
stand of a fast food franchise,

in a building whose very
lines launch rockets. Dark *Moderne*,

suck back your shadow. Blitz and
I, we've turned a bit to stone.

Follower, we know you well.
You are the future grown old.

The Goblin Market, or,
The Sorrows of Satan

The Southeastern Comic Book and Science Fiction Fair will be
held in Atlanta August 13–15.
—Atlanta Gazette

To bargain hopefully for dog-eared Marvels
Come a stutterer of twenty-nine,
A deaf mute ten. And if the flesh has evils,
Here, in the epic sweep of sword and pen,

Are not the extra syllables subtracted
So the silence can add a tongue?
Ur-hero in whose image, much collected,
These your servants are not made, among

Your Ur-er, more heroic acts, give up
For once omnipotence, the role of prompter;
Deign to know, yourself, the unmoved lip.
Consider: if I promise, I your tempter,

All the world and tights that never crease,
How will you answer dumb, get thee behind me.
You will not? Well, if you need to ease
Clay feet, I shoe them. You know where to find me.

Meanwhile, be that speech of last appeal
To trade for whom the barterers must come.
The stutterer can say "Adida deal";
The mute lips move, around their chewing gum.

A Dialogue with the Bride of Godzilla

Accent Australian; "You speak English, no?"
Miss Sally Bowles has come to Tokyo.

Tight perm somewhat the worse for New South Wales,
Tie wrinkled by these two days on the rails.

We ride the club car. She's its Choo-Choo-San;
I am a camera—as, in Japan,

Who isn't. "Leica smoke?" tries Axis Sally.
Take up the opening or blind the alley?

"You must be an airline hostess."
                                        "Me?
Not hardly. I'm a nectress." (Ectually?

A girl who can't say Noh?) "But . . . how much call
Have they for redheads?" And so very tall.

"Oh, they don't *see* me Love, or I'd have qualms.
I dub the ingenues in monster films.

I've been seduced, kidnapped, all of that bother,
By Godzilla, Rodan, even Mothra,

Poor old dyke. Straight gin's a root back. *Rout* back."
That route, I fear, is Weimar via Outback.

"Did you like Kyoto?"
                                "Liked it there;
The trip's been tedious. I have to share

With some old bag who's got the berth above."
"She's in the diner. She won't *see* us, Love."

Imputations

The poppy carries into time
Its squalid link with opium,
The rose its colors of the wars.
Who, on the brokers' trading floors,
Has seen a tulip frenzy? Debt,
Greed, speculation blossom yet,
And in the waxen bud not one
Suggests itself. The frenzy's done;
If in the morning light the look
Hints still at bubble, if it broke
It would not bankrupt, only say
Enthusiasms have their day.
The morning turban, wide, noon crown,
Quick tangibles, go up and down,
As though mild breezes studied trends,
So our instruction were their ends—
A Dow Botanical, where bronze
Is up, gold down, and either warns:
No totem wholly without tribe;
No value some will not ascribe.

Page from a Bar Guide

In glassy ice, erect
And formal and exact
As any Christmas tree,
The juniper, *esprit*
Inviolate and form
Confined, has prisms. Norm,
Freak, diagram, its spines
Convert the sleet to tines.

And, blue of ice on blue
Of berry, fast accrue
The cedar flavors, taste
Of freeze. They do not haste,
Our days of Gibsons, roses,
But they come, whose spruce
Is in glass still. November's
June; the gin remembers.

Wine from the Cape

There will greet you at the end, Vasco,
Blood, and as its recompense this vintage:

Light of skies that flint the glass with gold;
Spray, as of seas, to fill the stem with cold.

The measured seasons of the land and grape;
Their compressed forces that as foam escape.

For all your daring and for all your loss,
A little wine that snares the Southern Cross;

That as a sapphire keeps one star alive,
Within the glass repeats its four, its five.

The Aswan Rowing Club

Above the dam the Nile at pool
Sits idle, and below that dam
It idles too. Cool afternoon
And the insistent *accents graves*
Of the feluccas give alone
A sense of movement. From a small,
Moderne construction on the shore,
Incongruous, but no more so
Than stereo on minarets,
Move out to break our brilliant still
The Aswan Crew: in their lean shell
Congruity of stroke, of time,
Of place, for all their hint of Cam.
The megaphone is not a drum,
But oars are oars, and in their beat,
In little, are the galley, slave,
The distant sweats of Actium.
Muezzin, coxswain, local crew,
The triumph you enact is you.

Eniwetok Mon Amour

Yerkes Primate Center has a population of laboratory animals
exposed to atomic radiation in the nuclear tests the military con-
ducted in the 1950s, an experimental resource that could no lon-
ger be assembled.

—Annual Report

The lab technician is an entrail reader
Late to own it; science a restraint
That cages for us future on the hoof—
Curt life forms that will mutate and will speak,
Or that will keep their peace and reassure.
Already, in the nations of the cage,
Destruction gathers or does not; the ape
Grows old uncancerous, and if he dies
Outwits us, as he has no issue. Flies,
For all we know, have bred the danger out
Long since, and are our fruit's destructive heirs.
High Priesthood of the Pyrex and the knives,
For whom the seed of seeds, unstable still,
Is ripening to law, do not suppose,
If in the flesh irradiated, seared,
You find the image of the branching cloud,
It was not there before. The tree of blood,
The twisted prophecy you cut toward, is,
Unlikely augurers, not yet response;
Not the accusing, unambiguous
Mutation that you seek. It is the norm,
And what it says is: monster or to be,
For each if not for all, for flesh that waits,
The future is by definition monstrous.

Presence Française

(Tahiti)

The wind drops; uninflected off the screen-wire
Glance the trumpet notes. Has breeze a corpse?
Yes, just as barracks—red wire, copper-green wire—
Bury porch by porch the windy hopes,
The avaricious fevers of eclipse.

A bit of rust, a bit of patina . . . mesh,
However brittle, makes a winding sheet:
Algiers is here, Haiphong is, Marrakech.
In reveille, however, mess, retreat,
Grand-ducal Gerolstein survives defeat.

Better a bright, one-bugle operetta
Than a world as stations of the cross
Of Alsace and Lorraine. If vendetta,
Let it be the atoll's and the sea's;
Machetes sent against banana trees.

Scheherazade in South Dakota

Mitchell (1312 alt.) is located in the James River Valley and is
widely known for its Corn Palace, the only one of its kind in the
world. Entirely decorated in corn and products of corn, the exot-
ic-appearing structure was erected in 1921. The Corn Palace each
year attracts thousands of visitors from South Dakota and neigh-
boring states.
                    —Federal Writers' Project, *South Dakota, a guide*

Implacablest, remotest, levelest!
Immensest prairie, out of what false East

Have you created, dome and corn and spire,
The world of Rimsky-Korsakov entire?

Ill-mated as the nightingale and rose
The brick of Main Street and the *quelque chose*

It partners: all too visible Kitezh,
A Rimsky bauble, bead, and Bangladesh,

Or silent Baghdad of the elder Fairbanks.
Have shops, haphazard banks and doctrinaire banks

Financed it, or (have chickens change of sex?)
Did it their cockerel lay golden eggs.

It is that gleam that to the farm snow-maiden
Poses fresh careers as go-go maiden.

In the small town still it is a wind
That says "O wondrous land, O land of Ind."

The wind is gone; a whirlwind here and there
Clocks off the dusty time of one more year.

On Sindbad of the storefront time lies heavy.
Rimsky was a young man in the Navy.

Death and the Bush Pilot

Unmatching shadow paralleling me,
As, underneath my stubby fuselage,
The long pontoons pursue, or as the ski,

You final charterer, to what rivage
Must we intend, and from what shore embark?
Here where the buildings, like a double Taj,

Lie white in air and on the water dark,
Or from the granite shield? There, oval ice
All winter indicates the inlaid lakes,

And in the skies of spring pedantic geese
(O sauve qui peut, shy dove who taught the Ark)
Create one-letter alphabets, and pass.

Cendrillon
(Chateau Frontenac)

Godmother, you have altered all things else
And not transfigured me. My sisters' guilts

Speak English still, but if they twinge at all
It has not slowed their going to the ball.

Their progress is a chauffeured, pumpkin traffic
To lit chateaux Canadian Pacific.

This, the mother house (stepmother house)
Has scores of chimneys, more than one live mouse.

Roofline sharp and roofing copper-green,
Chateau, your press your everlasting lien

On each long adolescence, you the hearth
And you the ballroom. Suffering your dearth

Of belt or Disney powered mediators,
I mop your floors, I dust your radiators,

Sort your trash—a cinder separatist.
Someday my prince will come: a Jansenist,

Charmless as only Jansenists can be.
I date an English boy, and fleur de lys

He knows from crosswords as "Brazilian snake,"
As I know fer de lance is Union Jack.

Bilingualism cries "The hour's eleven!"
I feel middle-aged at half past seven.

Neither glass nor loss nor hope of ease,
The carpet slipper fits and is my peace;

Though, when the red brick turrets dip their flags
(The Maple Leaf, if one may say so, rags)

And in their chill June sky the stars are many,
I love the fairy tale as well as any.

Maeterlinck in Ontario

Yvonne ma soeur, ma soeur Yvonne,
From what hard dungeon are you won?

The state whose wards, whose prize we were,
Ma soeur Cécile, Cécile ma soeur.

Annette ma soeur, ma soeur Annette,
In what dim bondage are we yet?

The Church, with this result you see,
Marie ma soeur, ma soeur Marie.

And you our sister? In your grave
Are you our freedom? What you have

Immense and what you lack so small?
That little, O mes soeurs, is all:

A marriage that hides your name,
A child to wake you out of fame,

Your middle age that cossets you,
Your own yard, where the bird is blue.

No freedom mine, save, of this ground,
Its thorn; the ban, the spell regained,

And dreams in which forever pass
We five behind our wall of glass.

Via Spaceship through Saskatchewan

Another planet, or the look thereof:
High prairie featureless, high clouds aloof.

Above the summer air the arching frost;
In every breeze some hint of winter lost,

Of cold to come. Two seasons spread at once,
One sky whose quarters all are north, no tense

You negate dulls our flashing heaven, fights
Its mounting charges that will be the lights.

Invisible aurora, heavy wheat,
This other Saturn knows its ring is sleet.

And, cities of that planet's cautious plain,
The clustered silos elevate the grain.

At the Mercy of the Queen-Empress
(Victoria, B.C.)

Two grasses by the Empress hedge;
The one to smoke, the one to edge.

I lean a while upon the edger,
Smoke a joint, add up the ledger.

One week now I'm twenty-eight.
If I go home I'm not draft bait;

I'm not young either. Edgar Hoover,
All the smarts are in Vancouver.

Why did I come here? That town
I left was brown on brown, on brown;

So misted trees and sunny water
For a while did sort of matter,

Like the sunlit summer nights,
The great green dome outlined in lights.

It's summer over; statue viewing
Shows the Queen can stand renewing.

Summer's done; B.C., R.I.—
Whichever, Vic, it's soon goodbye.

You tourists on the morning ferry,
Hot tea cosies rest you merry.

You're that picture in the shops:
Rowboat and rower, stand-up corpse.

Don't look for lights; don't look for tinsel.
All ashore for Toteninsel.

Advice to King Lear

Arneson River Theatre, on the San Antonio River, is the most
unique of the city's theatres. On one side of the river are tiers of
grass seats; on the other a patio-type stage. Occasional passing
boats enhance audience enjoyment.
                                    —*San Antonio; A Pictorial Guide*

Unlikely in the semi-desert, azure
Night, the storm out on the heath is seizure
In the King's own madness. It is pressure
On the backers for a quick foreclosure.
Verse or wind machine, the awful matter
Finds its vehicle and has its stutter.

As if the footlights floated off in glitter,
Pleasure craft now part the placid water.
The onstage weather every act is glummer;
Outdoors or in, a mummer's still a mummer;
Your fool can only grow forever dumber.
Heirs? They march one to their different drummer.
Get on the boat, Old Man, and go to summer.

Ghosts

To Galveston among the oleanders
Mrs. Alving comes with Pastor Manders.

So transported from its fogs and fjords
Can fate grip? Do they hold, the silver cords?

Male nurse around the clock; a handsome trust fund.
She is valiant. It will be a just fund.

Here, also, some justice is. A heat
By 8 A.M. enough to drive out quite

Whatever glides among the local headlines;
Eager fury, unaware of bloodlines,

Stegomyia all the night. Yet, too,
Such mercies as has fifty. "I and you,

Hélène; our coffee made with chicory;
Palmetto fans, in their poor mockery

Of breezes."
                    "You and I, the Alving money;
Porch with, how to say, a Suck-the-?"
                                                        "Honey-

suckle vine. Put out the lamp, Frau Captain,
And come to bed." On shutters, swag, nets slept in,

The great mosquitoes light. But for the nonce
The furies wait; the lamp is in its sconce.

Anastasia

Anna Anderson Manahan

I am what you will.
Out of the cold canal

I come to seize my name;
Into its icy scum

I leap to shatter, once
For ever, consequence,

Selfhood, continuum:
I am not what I am;

I am. The missing corpse
Has presence on my lips;

Some peasant sense of wrong
Hangs silent in my tongue.

I, homing in on ease,
Prize catch of hostesses,

Know birth and what it does
Are brief as bleeding is,

Though madness and the scar,
Remaining what they are,

Weigh on me always. Past
Is that as which I'm cast,

And present (aye the rub)
My U.S. country club.

Far in the lime-white well
I lie and know no ill;

Hard by the cold canal
I stand as you too shall.

The Miller

Without imagination, but with long,
  Sure knowledge
I release the arms and set the sails.

He, heir of reading much and meaning well,
  To tillage
Alien and to the soil unknown,

Climbs on his mare. The wind turns back his charge;
  A servant
Waits always to blunt the folly's edge.

It is incompetence the future hails:
  Gaunt, antic.
I, meanwhile, grind the grain and feed two fools.

A Distant View of the Chinese Wall

Alien navigators whose deep space
Is dark behind you, bold automata
Who focus randomly whatever disc,
Whatever grid you have for telescope,
How will you, orbs, interpret these: an asp
Of stone by day, a graph of sparks by night.

Out there in your eternal present, probe,
You must well realize the wall you see
Is of a past the burdened light transports.
Can you envision, cores, incurious
Investigators of a nearest void,
The crowded time of garrisons and fires?

Of raging signals heaped up one by one
To urge our message toward the towers east,
Old wars the moving dots across your screen?
Know you the nomads of the isohyet?
How the wall defines it, and the rain
Obtains no more beyond? Adventurer,

Eye who exist in helmet or in head,
Lens, do you come, as sentry everlasting,
To identify with all who watch?
Or where you see a planet gone to dunes
Stretch west of Kiayükwan, the jade last gate,
To land and be as alien as they?

A Salutation to the Moons of Saturn

Bodies who tell the possibilities
Of desert, count the kinds of airlessness
And are a cold monotony that orbits,
To the yellow god you circle say,
However represented, we are breath:
Binary in-and-out that is the source
And self of what, in so well-armored form,
Is come to scan you. We have too a god,
Who are the temple he inhabits. Name
Him we cannot, although his many-lettered
Tetragrammaton is restlessness.
The planet that we live on is not large,
But, as you see, is not the whole. In blue
Air changed as wind and brightened for our sky
That still, that dark we share is tempered. Answers,
Dead exemplars in whom, ice and dust
(Our future, you or you), we know the Earth
For what it is, permit us, as we name
You waste, to know no more than heretofore
How, in the circle of our distant blue,
We dwell as in a warm oasis, whole
Of vanity and ignorant of need.
Hail, Titan, and allow us leave to pass.
Scarred patricide of Time, the wilderness
You are rounds out for us what we are not.

News for Loch Ness

The Great Salt Lake is at its highest level in sixty years, and threatens surrounding territories.

—AP

A golden angel, rigid in the lifeless water,
Trumpets silently, green deeps his judgment come.
Salt, more and more an architect, a water Goth,
To all the Temple's major pinnacles adds minor,
Benchmarks when the Lake is Bonneville again.
Down to the triple spires, that glitter in the grains,
Equipment of the treasure seekers drops and lights.
Long pikes break in the crusted doors; the veil is rent.
Nowhere the vessels; robes are not, nor any gold.
Faith hid them in the granite mountain, with the names.
Outside the orbit of the diving helmets, name
Without a genealogy and life for salt,
Leviathan engenders: "Bonnie," of the Lake
Its legend guardian, a symbiont of gulls.
The trumpet sounds; salt moves; the giant tail sweeps by.
And, effigies in leaking shrouds, iron masks, torn tubes,
A marriage of air, the plunderers lie sealed.

The Chinaberry Tree

Its shape uncertain in the bloom that scrims it,
Purple, and itself a haze of gnats,
The tree that will be knowledge, or what seems it,
Beckons in the rising heat and waits.

Its shade will feather, and be serpent; there,
Instinct to take the field and meet the beast,
Are bound, already bargainers, a pair
On whom the subtleties will all be lost.

The altered apple, as if randomly,
Exerts its blunt appeal, and though who fall
Acquire a taste, it is not learning. Try,
Avenger, angel posted, as you will.

The sword that flames exile shows up to be
Dessert stuck on a skewer, and the taint
Of Adam, late and early, gluttony.
How tartly, as the sandflies learn, the faint,

Soft blossoms harden in their unmeant Eden
Toward the green, emetic berry: scent
Nil, outline clear—late come-on for a want
Too uninformative to seem forbidden.

The Consultant

To the original design? No. None-
theless it easily can be completed.
Will it reach the sky? To the extent
One's concept of it does. So, in a graph,
Our curve approaches, but the touch eludes.
Though in a driest air strict clouds should form
Below its summit, past its pinnacle
The envied blue lies open, in whose reach
Intent is all, and dialogue well lost.
Come, let us make a name. Exact the brick
And tax the glaze. Another set of plans,
A little scaffolding . . . your money lenders
Will extend you. Nothing we imagine
Shall we be denied. For driven flesh
Height's endless ramps already wait. Doubt not
The brow, the sweat to be forthcoming. Send!
Command itself need be your only tongue.
It is the inching promise that will speak;
Not only to the cognizant of charts
Do glare and triumph beckon. From an Earth
Upon whose face are scattered in full gesture
All who seek a lingua franca still,
Await you, loud, your legions. What you have,
For now, is failure to communicate.

Seeking a Level

Omnipresent in the Hanging Gardens
    Falling water.
Stair of stairs and vine of vines, a stream,

A sound, descends the stepping blood: Euphrates
    Raised to heaven
To become the ditches of the tiers.

The morning cataract pours off its cornice;
    Noon has dried it;
In the afternoon the lower basins

Shine with amber of a sand accruing.
    Now, in the evening,
Climbing as the setbacks one by one

Scale off to darkness and the upper courses
    Soar in sunlight,
Come the gardeners to light the lamps.

Leaf, wick, leaf. Fire, the final fruit, breaks open,
    Upward cluster
Weightless at the cotton of its stem.

The newest, nearest leaves in pairs are parching;
    In the siphons,
Soon, the muddy artery renewing.

Is it the highest terrace that is greenest?
    Or, fed with time,
The roots at bottom where the water falls?

To the Lighthouse

Pharos, where the farther night
Surrounds in one smooth line a sea
We center, roughened in the oars . . .
You, as we see you first, are fire
Inside a cloud; are, as we near,
A lightning our horizon traps.
High mirror hot behind the fire,
For cordwood carried to your height,
For terraces of windlasses,
The duty rosters they enchain,
We have no feel, though we ourselves
Are mere extensions of our oars.
Egyptian slavers of the flame,
Our thanks. Deep drum who time our stroke,
Be thunder of their guiding flash,
As each great windlass-handle is,
In threat of storm, direction, hope,
Unfailing oar to row us home.

Great Diana

Ephesians whom your idol paupers,
Worshipers who feed the hundred breasts,
Are you their servants fed in turn?

For what you bring, for fire and specie,
For these melons and for work of hands,
Does she the goddess, venal judge,

Hand down to you in ivory gestures
All you long for and your sense of worth?
A future for your name and blood,

And for your vanity a nipple
Named as yours? Its suck withdrawn is self
Forgot; is arrow and the wound.

Herself the crescent of her forehead,
She the huntress ever at the full,
The breast she burns is too the bow.

Deception as she wanes and waxes,
Is she, to your cost, as well the Earth?
Or, selfish of her way, the world

Merely: intolerant of challenge,
Envious of yield. Her Ephesus
Of tribute, city that you paid,

Goes under in its time of earthquake;
Temple quarried, mysteries borne off,
Contour of her fecundity

In fetid melon vines is captive.
Did she, as the circle of her breasts
Spun free and eons in her womb

Aborted, seem a blaze she enters
In some future pregnant to return?
And did the gold whose shaping seams,

Whose tension held in just position
Ivory that was the idol's form,
As melting mass become the self,

Soul, service of who now inherits?
Is it logic that for us, for now,
Brute Mammon is her only birth?

After the Fall

In water shallow, but enough to cover,
Prone the once colossal lies;
And we who are expression in his eyes,
As swimmer and as iris, diver

Centered in wet lids' surrounding copper,
Are we here for more than scale?
To be comparisons who where he fell
Unblind him with a mask and flipper?

True, his sight cannot be ours;
Aberrant sunlight slipping through the dapple
Is for him his loss of force;
Dark countercurrent strong. He was Apollo.

Green colossus by another harbor,
Lords us, in a sun god's crown,
Divinity our own. Our blindest fervor
Lights her torch; a swimmer's arm,

Upraised, exaggerates her strident gesture.
She the world she now bestrides—
Upright the more to topple all—a posture,
And no more, us she corrodes.

Relics

Let what the dogs will leave be flesh enough:
You will inherit saints adored on less.
Authenticate me, dripping palm of hand,
And hope, high lacerated arch, warm sole,
That in the crystal case to which you go
Who kiss you taste a dust of Jezreel.
Torn lips laid back from alternating teeth
Cannot announce if I was saint or no,
Nor wheel of chariot uncanonize.
Two ways, Jehu, to meet the conqueror:
To scrub the cheeks and vanish in the crowd,
Or, when the eunuchs huddle near one's back,
Who plot the envoy envy pays to power,
Beside the sill to line the eyes anew
And face the scavengers, the pavement down.
Have at me, curs. Beyond the worst you do
Time still will know me as its painted face.

Elijah of the Backward Glance

Out of the past to feed the prophet
Come, for the time dependably,
Heat's unselective ravens: surfeit
Half-recalled in beaks of dates
And famine on dry combs foretold.

Far wings who bring us desert honey
And who pass the date-palm by,
Tomorrow when the bread is stony
Will you bring us still—bright bits
Of mirror—broken years to hold?

Or, turning on the skull you succor,
Peck the tongue that, going dry,
Eats any glass. Crow, scarecrow, plucker-
Out who as the vision cuts
Hold high the speech you fear, be bold:
Age will not scorn your dusty sweets.

I the Swineherd

To their destruction out of sight
Go past at speed the Gadarene:
Their labored demons each one trite
With common swinishness—obscene

The many as the one was not.
Love, did I so run after? Greed,
Were yours these cliffs that speed the gait?
Have pity, Precipice. The need

Grows weaker, and who lived to wait,
To guard, to hope to discipline
Soon learns. He learns his trust was bait.
It vanished, his vocation's gone.

Our Lady's Juggler

The miracle is mine, My Lady.
Do not think your lifted hand,
Your so late simper count. The steady,
Prompted poise of no hoops in the hand

And some hoops in the air surpasses.
This I make for you of rest,
Eye, wrist—a going magic—grace's
Access neither harms nor much assists.

Grace is to have no need of grace,
And I who send out no prospectus,
Leave no memory, give phase
To fall, in giving mass my little ictus.

In the Kingdom of Jerusalem

Secular heirs of spirit's little hour,
We govern in the aftermath of frenzy:
Ordered watches where the Crusade ends.
Between the Dead Sea and the live, our narrow,
Alien land. We signal, and the torch
Is for the shore levant, as its response
Is for the desert fastness the decline.
Two fires our width, our panic, our defense.
Who guard the shrines, add terraces for grapes,
Exploit the pilgrim, wed the infidel . . .
They (we) back up against the evening star.
Near Hesper, newest bulwark out of Europe,
Flash from shore to sand the flickered strength.
As, when the flood recedes, the salt is structure,
We, fore retrospects of brimstone fall,
By margin castles pillar-up the dawn,
Who glisten by the fact of shrinkage. Heap,
Rear Guard, the brazier high; and if from star
Nor West no answer comes, assess your creed.
The zeal that brought you here must buy you off.

Rex

Fools, Milord, but is it feast?
Are they fed, these whom you misrule?
How appetite itself is beast,
And is its satisfaction. Fool,

King, poor transported head of plaster,
Had you body save this pike
That jabs you fresh toward fresh disaster
Might less narrow passion speak?

Or is the faceless that you are?
The bladder's mask and body's vizard,
Mocking what it goes before.
Lead on, Blind Dunce. One feeds on hazard.

Favors
(Including an Egg Timer)

Comus who end the carnival,
Largesse who on your float of treasures
Bear the gifts we seek, let fall
Such trinkets as will be our futures.

Give, but give without distinction.
To the luckless fling the dice,
And to the cured of fever, unction
In its waxen phial. Toss,

To all the young and warm of flesh,
The china skull to chain their keys;
To all who cough the tray for ash.
To who are old a sand that flees;

Unto each cripple canes of candy.
It is we who take the toss
Who sort the lots that we shall end,
In time, without or with. The loss?

Who has the limp must time the egg.
Dip, therefore, to who bargain, Comus,
Yours the cup: libation quick
To slow the timer, spare, unmaim us.

The Space between the Andirons

Only ash may fully be implicit,
May in bright beginning fire be end.
Front smooth who in the antlered god lie tacit,
Impediment who on his tongue portend,

You fine obscurity (how clear!) to whose
One soot the coroneted flame will come,
Allow it, that is godhead of our use,
So long to lord as, discontinuum

Between the dark and dark, it is not form
But form eluded: now the lick that forks
And now its undivided answer—storm
Before the calm, and in the heats of sex

A branching sconce of other sex that waits.
Sustain, undifferentiated fall,
Upon our hearths the sparkling marquisates,
High, blazing earldoms to which flesh is thrall.

Below each bare, each hardly trophied mantel
Create forever new the ardent stag
And forehead sprouting; past the newest lintel
Illusion there is home, and tongues that speak.

Hurricane Lamp

In warm cut-glass the geometric fire:
Triangle the half or diamond the whole,
Unstable in the still the bright parts pair,
Vibrate, divide; as if to say the gale

Engenders in the eye, and in the wind
Are lapses where the fire can tower high.
New smoker of a charcoal filter, mind
You do not burn your fingers as you try,

Face lowered toward the bar, to suck the flame.
In vortices as calm, ineptness wrecks;
In proper lighters, in the wettest storm,
The hooded flint rolls sparks along the thumb.

Here, have a match. Its height two hands protect.

Adding Rattles

The season turns, and to its chillest blood
Bears witness that a skin must soon be shed:
The rounding self forsaken; with its scars,
Its old concealments worn to use, be lost
Also our shining tread that knows the earth.
Another year of clarities and shade
Demands its other dazzle to conceal,
And on our backs the diamonds are fresh.
Old Belly, can you learn again the ways
Effaced? And you, Blood each time more enclosed,
Can you account it, in so hard rebirth,
All gain that you should see beside you, stiff
In death and in this wisest light transparent,
What you were? Who gain here otherwise
(Warm!) no envelopment not still to lose,
And one more sound to warn each touch away.

So Here It Is at Last

News, boredom, debt, guile. All are borne, but all are crosses.
How to be a man of fifty cutting losses
  In the loss of nerve.

How very long ago, in simple confidence,
One took the day at hand as what would issue thence,
  And as the just dessert

Of act and its own past. Vague future, quick to come
And sure to disappoint the shape you shadow, numb
  Your coming with the sting,

The thrust of change: each hope you monster, year abort,
A nothing in our non-response—the drugged retort,
  The undistinguished thing.

The Alfano Ending

At the request of Toscanini and of Puccini's heirs, Alfano completed the unfinished third act of that composer's *Turandot*.
—*Grove's Dictionary of Music and Musicians*

Of that other person who began,
I have the work, to do with as I can.

All his imagined endings left undone
I must imagine and reduce to one,

That necessarily will be despised,
As even I know how the realized

Falls short of the potential. Instant mask
And lifelong cruelties I have the task

Of making viable. I see it out;
One earlier could leave the end in doubt.

You challenges I now would most avoid—
My given and my lack—the past deployed,

So intricately flight is either met.
Each riddle, Princess, has one answer: *stet.*

Therefore I do my mechanistic best
By love in which I have no interest.

Of hints and sketches, scenes scored long ago,
I fashion might-have-been and make it go.

A younger man (O time and time to spare!)
Set down these elements that are my care.

The grafted life I give another's say
Is no late masterpiece. But it will play.

Promises, Promises

The rain was real, that in the lashing water
Leaves its white unease, its easy spatter.
Neither truth nor force nor pitted glitter,

Fraud, the double rainbow gates and gates
Its high wet distance. Arch of violet,
Vague outer arch in which you bright are set,

The hope you portal is the air you are:
As little firm, as unparticular.
Faint colors general and nothing ours,

To each as each his end must here be sold.
The rain was real; be you a lie well told:
Air's seven colored bridge from gold to gold.

A Song for Clines Corners

Hitchhiker east, Hitchhiker west,
I wish you nothing but the best:

However Euclid may be loath,
A single ride to take you both;

A silent driver, never stopping;
Night and stars, and some stars dropping.

In your two guitars the wind,
That is your breath as it is thinned.

Yawn, light a cigarette, dream, doze.
East is East, and West . . . who knows?

Advancing night, forever later;
Meteors no more: a crater.

Dream or waken, I your host
Am at the end the endless coast.

The boatman waits; the plank is crossed.
Lift up your tongue and put the cost.